The Boy
in the
Labyrinth

AKRON SERIES IN POETRY

AKRON SERIES IN POETRY
Mary Biddinger, Editor

Titles published since 2010.
For a complete listing of titles published in the series,
go to www.uakron.edu/uapress/poetry.

Oliver de la Paz

The Boy
in the
Labyrinth

The University of Akron Press
Akron, Ohio

ISBN: 978-1-629221-72-4 (paper)
ISBN: 978-1-629221-73-1 (ePDF)
ISBN: 978-1-629221-74-8 (ePub)

A catalog record for this title is available from the Library of Congress.

∞The paper used in this publication meets the minimum requirements of ANSI/NISO
z39.48–1992 (Permanence of Paper).

Cover image: *Poetics of Skin*. Photography by Rosalyn Driscoll. Cover design by Amy Freels.

The Boy in the Labyrinth was designed and typeset in Minion with Frutiger display by Amy
Freels and printed on sixty-pound natural and bound by Bookmasters of Ashland, Ohio.

**Affordable
Learning Initiative**
THE UNIVERSITY OF AKRON

Produced in conjunction with the University
of Akron Affordable Learning Initiative.
More information is available at
www.uakron.edu/affordablelearning/

Contents

"I know what the Greeks do not know, incertitude."
—Jorge Luis Borges

"Neither living nor learning was good without order."
—Temple Grandin

"I have designed my style pantomimes as white ink drawings on black backgrounds, so that man's destiny appears as a thread lost in an endless labyrinth....I have tried to shed some gleams of light on the shadow of man startled by his anguish."
—Marcel Marceau

"Everything I've done, I've done for you. I move the stars for no one."
—David Bowie as Jareth in *Labyrinth*

Credo

Twenty-Eight Tiny Failures and One Labyrinth

***

Before I set out to write something about family or friends, I open with an apology. The apology is similar—"I'm sorry for writing this, but I have to," or something to that effect, and then it's deleted with the next line.

***

I have been writing the same sequence for almost eight years. I suppose that's not too long as far as works in progress go. But sometimes I feel like I'm chasing someone down a twisting pathway.

***

I grew up with allegory as a way to understand. This story can stand for this. This person is wicked. This person is good. This choice is flawed. This is a wise choice.

***

Two of my sons are on the autism spectrum. This pervades my daily life. We are supposed to "write what you know," and what I know and have known my ten years of fatherhood is that writing what I know is hard.

***

Meredith and I must've filled out at least a dozen questionnaires assessing this and that. We both found ourselves baffled at one point or enraged at another point. The questions felt somewhat accusatory. Like the boys were some case. Some project.

***

Labyrinthian. The paperwork was labyrinthian.

***

When I delete my apologies, I can imagine the words are still ghosted in the pixels of my screen.

***

When we co-slept with L he would dig his fingers right into our eye sockets.

***

I do not know what having total creative freedom looks like. I give myself tasks—duties. My rituals involve organizing my sensory planes, and lately organization has been impossible.

***

Human interaction is such a complicated thing. It is this complication which baffles my sons. Sarcasm. Subtlety. All the coded nods and micro-gestures of day-to-day interaction. A knowing glance. A smirk. An off-color joke. Labyrinthian.

***

My sons are having trouble making friends at school. They are each other's best friend and because of this they speak their own language to each other. N will pull L closer and loudly exclaim this or that about a video game. L will smile. They have an audience, and I'm pleased they have each other.

***

And how to articulate this as a writer and as a father? But as a father first?

***

L's obsession with eyes continued until he was four. I had been called in to his daycare a few times because he had poked one child or another in the eye.

***

I apologize for writing about you, L. I apologize for writing about you, N.

***

[   ]

***

Alicia Ostricker punched me sharply in the arm after I told her I wasn't writing about my kids.

***

Since 2013 I have been writing a sequence of poems loosely based around Theseus and the Minotaur myth. I do not name the wanderer of the maze. The wanderer of the maze is simply "the boy."

***

I realized that I had been writing about my sons for several years in the form of this allegory.

***

This is unclear to most readers.

***

Sometimes it's important to keep secrets.

***

You don't have to "see" to know.

***

Here's a fact: I have written 100 "Labyrinth" poems. Here is another fact: I wandered in their maze without understanding them for almost six years.

***

Here's a fact: I am getting older and my wife is getting older, and we acknowledge that our sons may not be able to care for themselves when we are gone. Here's another fact: that understanding keeps me awake at night.

***

I remember rubbing my eyes after a fitful sleep. I remember looking at Meredith and seeing cuts from fingernails on her lids.

***

I'm writing what I know.

***

I also know this—I don't want to be the person who fixes this version of my sons to the page. This understanding keeps me awake at night.

***

I wanted to understand my sons as well as a neurotypical parent with his own limitations and his own biases can understand a neurodiverse child. I am full of flaw and misconception. I am full of error.

***

And so is the language at my disposal to articulate an experience not mine.

***

I apologize for writing about you, L. I apologize for writing about you, N.

***

[   ]

***

Prologue

Minos

Soft, the summer air. Another August's dark-ale sunset.
The stillness is unanswered in the temple, despite the woven garlands,

the grains, the gems, the crates of fish strewn about the polished floors.
Perhaps the voice of the god is quiet like a bowstring drawn tight

or as a love which is secret. Perhaps the voice is the inarticulate sound
of water on rock. Still, the bull's horn shines bright and clean

like a spinning needle. The beautiful sons and daughters of Athens
are before the king, chained ankle to wrist, ankle to wrist, and

in the descending sun are bolts of yellow silk. The great halls
of Cnossus are rimed with a nimbus of flies but the marble stays
    unbloodied.

There is something the king had forgotten—something as unbearable as
    grief
upon which nothing was written. His mouth is not a delicate scroll

nor the sting of a black wasp with an unfurled paper nest. Just below
his watery eyes, the shadow of the maze and of the beast, for a single

breathless moment, held still between candlelight. The past is a shawl in
    a storm,
tangled in the branches of a willow. The scrims of light a remnant fear.

Blacker than the earth's first pitch, the eyes of the bull drink in
the torches. The white fire teases his matted hide. Each burgundy hoof

clacks on the cobbles, and his spiral horns reflect light at odd angles.
The only altar is rough stone, and no god is appeased by this offering.

There is no swift and merciless justice here except the thought that
  sometimes
what's miraculous is what's purely human. The king and his perfect
  world

wander through the labyrinthine hallways, mad, searching for the blood
  of the young
while the father's beast gives back the black hearts to the depths which
  are blacker still.

Strophe

Autism Screening Questionnaire:
Social Interaction Difficulties

1. Does your child have poor eye contact? Does he stare from unusual angles?

Yes. Like a dark bird from a high perch.
Yes. With acetylene torches lit somewhere in the distance.
     With eyes wide as the Morpho's iridescence.
Yes. Wild and hot like fixed stars.

2. Does your child not seem to listen when spoken to directly?

We call it dappled thoughts. He is constantly dappled—
here and not here. He is a thrush hidden in the sage.

3. Does your child have excessive fear of noises? Does he cover his ears frequently?

With wind there are moments—agonies. Like the time
we found him covering his ears in a cement sewer pipe
during a storm or when he fled into the street, shocked
by the vacuum cleaner. Often we hold him hard to keep the world
from flooding in. Often the world is sirens.

4. Does your child seem like he is in his own world?

We mourn him daily. And yet he guides me by the hand
through the threshold of his room as one guiding someone
just off a train, gently and lightly, avoiding the gap between
the platform and the track. The heat from his hand,
combustion-warm. Old stove in which we've heated this house.

5. Does he lack curiosity about his environment?

Because the color of the red door renders it mute.
Because the color of the die-cast car is an empty blue
and the sound of our voices could be any possible starling
we are not here. He is not here. And what of the place you reside
if you don't reside in it? Where then does your body blink?

6. Do his facial expressions not fit situations?

Nulled into a thick disquiet. Mouth agape.
Agate of the eye catches quick the inseam and
no blemish. No, no turning away and no smile.
The contraption shuts its winking gap.

7. Does he cry inappropriately? Does he laugh inappropriately?

A soothing so honed it does not surface
or salvage the daily losses. Which are also sharp
vibratos of hums along the jawbone—the music's
arrowing shot into the thalamus. A strobe's command
and call. A conspiratorial ache.

8. Does he have temper tantrums? Does he overreact when he doesn't get
his way?

He is a dark and stabled bull kicking at the chained gate.

9. Does he ignore pain? For example, when he bumps his head, does he
react?

If it strikes you can't rescind it. Juncture to
the brain. Sharp cortical hurt into which

leap charges—synapse to synapse, but then what?
A question asks its question. A hurt insists and yet.

10. Does he dislike touch? Doesn't want to be held?

There's something about proximity. The dutiful
belonging of atoms and how we relate to
the world through our skin. The exposed parts
of ourselves and how those pavilions are brushed by
a plum tree's wicked thorns.

11. Does he hate crowds? Does he have difficulties in restaurants and super-
markets?

Every day he's praying through the meanwhiles.
The sequences of. Not just aflutter, but alone
he sits on the periphery. Ears beside his little body.

12. Is he inappropriately anxious? Scared?

To soothe, the sound of humming through teeth. And so
a symphony of fears. The ventricular outbursts pleat
the clouds. The sky is always exploding
and in that delirium, a curdled tone.

13. Does he speak the same to kids, adults, or objects?

Remind us of our asymmetries. Who is that again? And what
smile to let the darkness in? I see him speak to the man
in blue work clothes and the way his face yields to
the light. To the way moments like this explode.

14. Does he use language inappropriately (wrong words or phrases)?

The world is a network of minds. Think
of the tongue and the fibers that make
its muscles. The branching capillary network
enmeshed. Alive and cooled with a song
that slides away. Tongue jammed in its stirrup
thinking of itself and the blood-red
amanitas pushed out of the earth.

Chorus: Complete the Sentences

Collapse into the short, _____ breaths. Something mouthy like a vapor from the empyreal blue fabric, freshly laundered. That is the taste of it. The hydrangea's bud opens into tongues. Like the little _____ undoing little buttons, one wound at a time.

A. Parenthetical...pucker
B. Elliptical...sips
C. Sensate...jabs
D. Insensate...thrusts

Episode 1

Labyrinth

The boy in the labyrinth holds a torch before him. He cannot see his shadow, which behind him swims in a somnambulant glaze. Winds tighten around the boy's body and his torch so that the universe lowers its eye to this den beneath the earth. Blossoms of fire flit from crevasses. The boy thinks, to be guided through the labyrinth is to be guided by bodies filling with light. The universe thinks, there are the stars. There and there and there.

He feels the ball of twine unspool from his hand. The soft speed of its spill-age as he walks. He measures it; his intimacy with its heft. The knowledge it erodes as spring water through quartz. Down the passageways, a game of cat's cradle tugs itself into a bright red web. In the darkest dark, the red twine twists about the corridors. It breathes the way a heavy sleeper breathes. Soon the boy in the dark has no string in his hand. To return to his demar-cations is to enter a thicket, to bind oneself to the ligatures of one's own making. The darkest dark takes a deep breath as the boy's hand feels for that which sleeps beside.

The boy hears the beast. The pad of the beast's hooves, quiet vowels sung to a sleeper. The boy listens to keep himself awake. He thinks of spiders on the edges of their webs, the ballet they dance on their self-made filigree. He thinks of an azalea sewn into the hem of a dress. The boy thinks, *this kind of thinking led me to the labyrinth.* Its black geodes. Its promises of wild crystal blooms held within. Morning digresses into night, and the beast's song laces its orbit through limestone causeways. It grows smaller and smaller until imperceptible. The boy soon misses the song. The beast's idle stroll. The faint breeze to remind that there is anything there in the widening dark.

The boy has been following his shadow. He conceives it to be god. And god said genius is in the eye of its wearer. God said the land before us awaits its innocents. The boy thinks he will sleep soon and that his shadow's tongue is lined with velvet. Above the two, stars and the blue heart of the moon threaded with its meteoric scars. God said this is a maze and your questions are hard. God said there are miracles and there are miracles. The boy thinks he will sleep soon and that his shadow is scrubbing the white from the moon. The boy thinks if he were to lie down, he and god would see doubles. And in the under-light of bright stars they both know the world they live in chooses them.

*

He is lost. And it is not by chance. He is here to find the beast, maker of accident and conservator of bones. At night, the boy listens to his body. The gardens of blood along his carotid. The march of his pulse into the blue garlands of his wrists. What a terrible place to lie awake and listen, he thinks. Terrible, to be lost within the spirals of the ear. Somewhere, the beast keeps time with its paces, antechamber to antechamber. The sound of his horns rubbing against marble. In a darkness such as this, old countries and new countries die and are born. And the labyrinth's causeways kiss their darkness, long and hard. Its own eyes shut tight.

The boy falls asleep. At his feet, the lumber's dying light ambles down the passageways. He is bone weary. The campfire's cinematic death shifts the landscape into impossible silhouettes. Then out. The ricochet of the boy's deep breathing barely kicks up dust. His rabbit-wary doze inches out of his open mouth then back in. The darkness is a hook threaded through his eyelid. How many days has it been in the dark? Every corridor changes into the next corridor. Every sleep an extravagance borne out of torment.

He plays word games in the dark: *lost, last, taste, waste*. Inside his mouth, an invention of the body. The fricatives rub themselves against his teeth. There is a river sound sliding past the corridors. There is a beast sound. The imagined orbits of birds throw their weight against the boy's ear. In the alchemy of air and voice, the most familiar muscle sips its drink. The boy plays on, lips pursed as if trying to kiss the black, air arrows out, as he says, *When*. As he says, *Whet* and *breath*.

*

As he raises his arms above his head, the torch behind him projects the shadow of a horned monster. This dim abdication of the boy's shape makes the silence of the maze stretch its legs like a proud house cat. The horns rising out of what was the boy's skull are a dream. There are dreams, and there are dreams. The boy's shadow returns as he drops his arms to his side with a slap of his thighs. The rush of wind as his arms fall causes an ember to lift from the torch with a pop. Other shadows try on their shapes in the stutter of the torch's hungry machinery. Other shadows circle in the sovereignty of their forms.

The boy in the labyrinth hears all its sounds: the breath's translucent cellophane in the cold, water's uncurled parabolas with each metronomic drip, the stalactites shearing winds into discordant vipers, and in the far reaches, the Minotaur—his incongruence, a bass drum. In the labyrinth, a sound knows its place. There are fingers in the darkness, pushing the black keys hard on their mallets. And lo, the quiet is the most violent string. The boy stands still. Somewhere on the surface, electric fans on rows of office desks push their thrombotic hums. Somewhere reams of paper let loose their repetitions like faucets spitting sawdust. Here, the dark's homunculus pads about on its bare feet while the spiral of the ear doubles back on itself.

Chorus: Solve for X

Then nightfall drops its thread, soft. The X has a texture of linen and is a mouthful of cool.

X is hungriest when the sun is red from carriage dust and about to take its last drink in the sea. X is hungriest when it hears the lambs sent down call each other by name. And X is full of their syllables of remembering. In the dark, nerve endings—seeing possibilities without maps.

The stars are erased in the maze; thus, X is the only god. And blood rises to the lamb's throats. Their bleating—necklaces of song.

Episode 2

Labyrinth

The boy in the labyrinth feels his ribs. In the torch shadow they are dark increments: space, skin, space, skin. If there were sound, its notes would flash against his chest like a scale, climbing upward into his brain. And thus the tortured walk up the spiral stair. Yet, in the labyrinth, there is no song for his ribs, save the gnaw of bone on cartilage. A rusted hinge. His fingers climb their edges like ecstatic dragonflies shuffling their wings, frenzied against the light. The strange fizz of his fingers' touch, a buzz amid the quiet between breaths.

He feels his fear. It runnels down his back as long as his breath lasts. He stands still in the darkened arch. Within him, a vowel—all curves and swallows. And soon a whistle sweeps the passageways as the Minotaur's hooves bayonet the ground. The bull-man walks as one in a dance. As one en pointe. His fetlocks catch the spark of hoof to cobble, and his cadence rebounds from wall to wall. Back against the smoothed stone, the boy closes his eyes. The slow riot of the Minotaur's steps wears the enamel from the boy's bones.

The boy finds a skull. He puts his hands over its eye sockets because there are wild flowers crawling out of the orbits. He brings his hands down so that they cover the nasal cavity and the mouth. And the skull kisses the boy's hand, bone hard. In the labyrinth there are nothing but the hardest kisses—and even if the skull's mouth lies...even if tonight the labyrinth talks the boy into crazy promises, pleas, little momentary apple blossoms, the keyhole opening of the nose can't smell the flower blooming forth from the sockets. The dead eyes can't see the shoot of the vine adoring itself.

So much waiting for the boy. Lights shift as hours pass—the mouth of the corridor darkens and lightens. Scenes moving at great speed. The boy's mind is a cinema. The projector's tongue snaps acetate through reels as the edge of the film unspools. But there is no film. Last silhouettes scuttle and exclaim the brevity of their daily dance. A tangle of spider webs sutures the growing dark and the only sound—this. The Minotaur sings.

*

The boy finds a cistern. He puts his feet in the water and watches the blind fish dart away, their pallid scales like flashbulbs. Breezes sweep off the water in a swirl as the cavern breathes a little. The air, a flavored velvet to the boy's hot tongue. The boy in the labyrinth wonders if this is where the Minotaur drinks. Whether other animals of the maze come down to bend their bodies here. To shake off the dust. To listen to the Minotaur's song. To fill their emptiness as water conspires with stone.

*

The boy makes a mask with his fingers by pressing his thumbs to his middle fingers for eyeholes. He looks through the spaces. For clarity. In the darkness, he thinks he sees a doorknob's spherical elegance. Through a spider web lattice, he crosses. The resins of the web stick to his hands, still forming a mask. Remnants affix from one outstretched pinky to the other. A mask over a mask. And the spiders in the corner dance as they pull up the frayed strands. And the mask over the mask disintegrates into another parlor trick with the speed of the boy's gait. And the doorknob turns into spherical stones. And the stones fail to apologize to the boy, their bludgeoned faces reflected in the haughty dusk.

The boy smells the musk of the beast. It hangs in the arches of corridors, a heavy spiced foam. The pang of it singes the boy's eyes. He thinks of peppercorns crunched between his back molars, the flavor spiking up into his nasal cavity. The smell bursts into his eyes and they tear. Around him the things of the lair. A skull. A child's shoe. A matte of hair. Somewhere the beast lowers his head and sharpens the points of his horns against the labyrinth stone. Somewhere the beast cleaves the air with his scent. Here, his smell swirls about the bone-strewn alcove. The boy in the labyrinth lifts the bottom of his shirt up to cover his nose and mouth. And in the lair, the vortex of a presence spins its cyclone.

The boy carves a rose on his thigh. The demands of the carving, elaborate, like the composition of stadium rows viewed from above or the tiers of petals suggesting a function. A wave. The tears on the boy's face reveal his commitment to the form. The function of the carving—to keep him awake. As in sport or competition, stadia echo with applause. The athletes act in bright fashion with their arms and their legs. Their torsos gleam under coliseum light. The skin of the boy also gleams in its phenomenon of pain. Radial petals steeped in his blood perform their actions gracefully. Who will clean his thigh? He wonders the truth of his condition. He wonders where the beast wanders, the plus or minus of in medias res. The predictability of a pattern. The configuration of lines returning to their centers.

The compass rose he cut into his skin swells—an impasto of blood and flesh. Infected, the lines of its design rise. The planes of the cuts' directions, separate spaces between. To the north, a scab-encrusted bridge. To the east, a hewn fold of skin like clouds over a mountain. Each point of direction its own landmark. And so on this small space of his body, the boy is many places at once. His leg, the architect of its own loss. Pain is its own company—the binary of mind and body. And the story of all bodies is anecdotal. The way a red spool of thread's unending repetition is guise for the mind's solitude. The way each cavern yaw spills its own antecedent.

Chorus: Light Is to Dark as Nerve Is to _____

Dazzle the cover with a potent sheen. Slips of it sheeting in high sides, the wax of it running along in lines. It coats the inside in a shell. When set ablaze, the fats bubble, pock the smooth vistas into moments.

Lesions into lairs where the air sleeps in the body's deep. And the nerves rise out of their sheaths, the ends extended like lips sucking in the air. The stifling air.

Episode 3

Labyrinth

The boy in the labyrinth hears hooves. He has entered the war gallery where the bones of warhorses hang from wires. Their bodies sway in mid-gallop as breathy winds from surface breezes leach their way through seams in the earth. The shiny equine teeth clamp on bits, and the boy imagines spittle streaks from their mouths down the length of their necks. The riders have ceased. Whip cords as shadowed hands from a hot lantern. And the spirit of their febrile hearts whistle between the spaces of rib cages. All the tunnels swallow sound except the pop-pop-pop of bone on bone. The flickering heart of the boy's torch painlessly flowers. Torch shadow and wind make them run. The misshapen gait of the horses...their mouths. The ghost of their tongues, mum.

The sound of rustling leaves—an impossibility, but still.... In the border between the organization of the maze and decay, there are autumn trees. The yellow ones hide behind the green ones. This is what he remembers of the surface world. If he moves his head fast enough, he can discern the whole structure of autumn. If he moves his body fast enough, he can understand the long moments between waiting. Like here, in the beast's nest. Waiting for him to come. The system of layers sinks from memory to memory, the way a racket of birds in the morning expands the empathy between two people. As though the beast and the boy were the only two beings in the world to hear it. The absence of others in a violent spark of sound. How the birds and leaves of thought acquire the arc of the beast's shape. The cave mirroring the mind. The boy, turning his head this way and that.

*

Flint on stone, the boy makes fire. The striations of ash from the twine…from leaves blown in, black smudges in the dust. Black marks announcing "here," and "here," and "here," to measure the accuracy of the boy's memory. The unconditioned desire of fire continues its story against the stone. The way it wishes for space and air. And therefore, heat. Therefore, the lost ways light in bright dissolving lines. Somewhere the heat naps the beast's hot fur, and the cauldron of what is the labyrinth boils with brightly lit intervals of twine. Somewhere the darkness. Somewhere the boy says, *I am here.* The beast says, *You are there.*

Heat from flames. Smoke curls. Wild tips of the fire brush his eyes that he closes until there are only slits of light entering his mind. In this way, he exercises control. Focuses on shaping fire by opening and closing his eyes. In order to master fear or in order to feel fear, the line between the mind and the mind succumbing to fire becomes the rasping sound of animals fleeing the cavern. The high squeal of bats and the breath of wings above. So in the fire, the boy closing and opening his eyes loses direction. The labyrinth, a kind of measurement as the heat sweeps across the boy's face. He turns. The labyrinth, an inventory of lives lapping by in the brief heat of the body.

*

The boy, water on his shirt, lifts the damp end over his face. His eyes, the only thing to be seen. He watches, walking backwards. The smoke turning on its belly, inching forward. Still, there are interruptions in the smoke's movement. Staggers. Little curls of time-lapse air. The intensity of the fire, an object, palpable in its manifestation. The irises in the boy's uncovered eyes trap the image of fire in a fixed and unspeakable repetition with each blink. As if the scene were on cellulose, each cinematic arc caught between the golden lines of eyelashes. The frame around it. The limits of it between the rift or the glimpse.

The boy makes a camera with his hands. His left hand's fingers coiled into a tube as his right cranks the imaginary reel into imaginary canisters. Light escapes the lens. Of few things the boy is certain as he films in the dark— sound, the way the nails of his fingers touch the nail of his thumb, the beast's smell as sharp as metal filings. Cranking the hand camera, the boy walks backwards. The fire he set glows beyond the corner. The beast roams somewhere beyond that. And somewhere in the imaginary canister of film, a blur of something against the maze's damp walls. Something mirrored. Stirred. Something—the labyrinth's blue walls. A reflection of the boy filming himself.

*

Lips pursed, he practices his kiss. He puts his palm to his mouth and lets his lips brush the tiny lines crossing this way and that. Something slings its weight from side to side and the boy stops. Doors swing their keyholes out as if to look. As if the swing of a door is hopefulness. As if the space once closed by doors presents the boy with a new overture. A movement toward love. Grimed, beyond the reach of his self-kissing, the boy wonders if the beast presses his face in his hands. Whether his palms are all rocket and flare. Moist from the beast's breath. Meanwhile the kiss in the boy's hand is noticeably hot. A coin warmed in the palm turned over and over again.

*

Water touches his face. Then heat. He remembers a storm. In the desert, the horizon darkens from monsoon, and jagged ropes of hail volley down from the clouds. The ice melts down his back in a single watery chord. Dribblings from the stalactites sink their teeth into the milky dark. Anything within the limits of his senses must be remembered. Must be held. Thus the common language of the maze. Thus the shock of ice at once cold and precise.

Shadows move with his torch, forming different animals. The bird. The rabbit. The dog. Aspects of the surface world. This makes him sad. The pain of seeing something beautiful, a physical form. Pain is a layer. Having spent a great deal of time in the dark, the shadows are multiples of beauty. Because there is a thickness to this beauty, the boy feels the weight on his heart. An internal presence of a word on the tip of his tongue. A word under a heavy geology, like the striations of rock. The stripes of rock shift under the shadows. The bird is flying. The rabbit is hopping. The dog is running. All of these shadows make him heartsick. Make him hum.

*

The beast stands in an underground stream, water pulling at the hairs of his legs in the darkness. And here, the beast sings. He sings with latitude, as if he is hurling wrens into the corners of the maze. The boy thinks, to describe the song is to take advantage of their relationship. What exists between them is his desire and his desire which is both obvious and opaque. The water must be cold, and the boy clusters a string of anecdotal details— the beast wears scraps; there are seams in the labyrinth which give off light; as the beast sings he closes his eyes. Because it is not possible for the boy to absorb this without being seen, the boy feels a deep unease. Because he cannot focus his attention to a point. Because he cannot look into the beast's eye while he sings.

Chorus: Select an Answer

A. You know the story of the sound—how it ascends like a silver balloon. Its skin, unbound from any limb taps the ceiling. Its hollow center hollowed still, through no alteration or repair.

B. The sound of it an inquiry into what is granted. And what is granted is the now. The now when a mallet strikes a tiny drum and what was once silent rises into the wide and white vowels.

C. The white vowels alone.

D. The dark cave alone.

Episode 4

Labyrinth

The boy in the labyrinth sees daylight. Its streams veiled by a rain of dust motes. Looking up, the boy feels he is on the ocean bottom. There, in that skittering, a flock of birds become manta rays. They pull their arms downward, and in the interval between strokes, a chance. With a mouth full of mimicries, the boy calls their song, spontaneous as the bitten part of desire. The cloven hooved part. The part that happens within the Minotaur's hum. Its songs spiral out of its mouth. Bright globes of air rise in forceful inattentions.

Wrens disappear into a clutch of small marks in the sky. The space between them, its own life force. There below the surface of the world, the boy cannot shake his transitory feeling. How the image of the birds fading into the light does not involve him. Wave after wave of liquid images, the spectral waters on a steaming horizon. The boy touches his skull and feels the minerals of his bones. He marvels at how the bluish light surrounds him. Soaks him while the maw of the corridors swallows the margins.

Clouds float above, dividing into smaller clouds. Parting as they do, they know no loneliness. They needn't reply to anyone. They just burst apart. Seams tugged by someone's hand. The boy does not know home, only its omission. And by omission, the sky is slathered by a deep and inky brush. The violent strokes, smears of plumage from a flock of rooks. The seams come apart. The fabric separates into two layers. The here and the here.

*

The boy sits with his knees to his chest. The sky—so far. In his chest, the isthmus between here and not here tugs its knot through the heart muscle. A heavy lub-dub sparks its tiny fire. His eyes on the sky and his body aflame on the inside. Still, the only real crisis is the keening of the beast as it flits somewhere between an actual orbit and the boy's imagination. The beast is in an elsewhere place. A place full of harmonies and dark. And yet, the boy's iris full of light cannot represent forgetfulness or the forgotten. The peculiar quality of the sky and the beams coming at a slant depict an aspect of time. A duration of loss.

*

He sees another boy in the sky. The boy above the labyrinth has a face full of shadow. A face obscured as the sun shines from behind so that the shadow from the boy above the labyrinth covers the face of the boy in the labyrinth. Above and below. And between the two boys a heavy breath. Between them, a chasm of darkness passed as though their tongues had passed a small stone from each to each. *You are a boy,* says the boy in the labyrinth. The boy above the labyrinth says nothing. A long silence between the two. *Send for help,* says the boy in the labyrinth. The boy above does not move. The boy beneath the boy in the sky is covered in shadow.

The boy is covered by the shadow of another boy. The outline of a head obscures the sunbeam. And in so doing, the boy in the labyrinth is within the shadow of a head as though he were the inner-working parts of that head. *I am the brains*, says the boy in the labyrinth. The boy in the sky says nothing, only shakes his head from side to side. *You cannot get rid of your brains*, says the boy in the labyrinth. Above, the boy in the sky covers his eyes and thus, the shadow of his arms becomes part of the shadow of his head—his shadow looking as if it had grown its own arms. Within the shadowed head and arms, the boy in the labyrinth says, *I am the boy in the labyrinth. And within you, watch me swim.*

In the one bright spot he looks up. He sees the shadow boy. The sky boy. The boy who looks and says nothing. A long silence passes between, as has always been their relationship—the silence between mouths like a set of empty parentheses. Evening and morning and evening again. Time in the maze is as time is out of the maze. Leaves appear, brighten, and disappear into peripheries. And into the yaw of the underground caverns, autumn in grand and blustery gusts. The boy and the boy not speaking. Only their mutual shadows. From above. From down below. And upon their mutual silence, the black breath of the beast fills the gaps between their parentheticals. In vaporous bursts, the hot snort of the Minotaur churns the calm.

Circles of hot breath swirl and swell. There is a boy in the sky who steadies his gaze and a beast wheezing in the black. Deep in the earth the breath stirs up smells: sulfur, earth, every noxious root splitting the seams of crust. The boy in the labyrinth feels the eyes of beings. Steam against his back shifts the torch flame from side to side. The shadow of a motionless boy, there aloft in the sky. The boy in the labyrinth thinks it strange to be the center of attention. Thinks it odd, the way the geodes catch light's furtive glances. The way the pitchblende hardens the dark.

Chorus: Complete the Sentences

After the first taste of the stone, the glands fire their dazzling salvos. A kind of pain, red like a pomegranate. Salt wants to be whatever salt wants to be. Sometimes the _____ between the jaw and the shoulder. The savory skin dragged with lavender so the sway of its taste is both salt and bloom. Both lagoon and ravishment. And to the lips, the systole runs back over its wound, and fever, sweet fever, walks its way into that _____ yaw.

A. landscape...stunned
B. chasm...marred
C. crater...jagged
D. distance...dizzying

A Story Problem

There are 100 yards of string laid out in a straight line and every 10 yards a flower sprouts from stone. The flowers are A. Red. B. Fuchsia. C. Yellow. D. White. E. None of the above. If a boy walks down this path and it is summer and he hums a song from childhood, will he pick A, B, C, D or choose E? Will he smell D's metallic hook and think of how gardenias are loudest in the heat? If the string were to tie back the scent could it? Could the string hold back whatever fire rises from A? The split hearts of B? Would there be enough string left to get the boy from X to Y to Z, which are not flowers but points like pinpricks on a map? And would someone be waiting for him at Z with a bouquet of gardenias and marigolds? Is there a field at the end of the street, wild with flowers and vines? And what of the map with names like forgotten flowers? What about E and how these are all bad choices? How the names in front of us are never right?

Antistrophe

Autism Screening Questionnaire:
Abnormal Symbolic or Imaginative Play

1. Does your child flap his hands? Does he self-stimulate?

In ecstatic moments, it is a kind of remembering
the body is the body. For example, these arms
are for grasping. These hands are capable of
holding and touching the known and unknown.
And how remarkable it all is—scintillate the way
wonder surges toward the filaments.

2. Does he bang his head?

On the inside, the retort of feeling accumulates
as weight. It is like the smoke that had risen
to the cellar suddenly becomes thick and resinous.
A song heard while submerged in a pool.

3. Does he self-mutilate? Inflict pain or injury?

Huddled close against the soft thrum of rainfall against
our roof and his fingers hook into my eye-sockets. It is always
this: his fingers seek an empty to fill, chorus
of his nails pressed into my flesh thrust into the seam
of our borders. My body. His pain. Our pain.

4. Does he toe walk? Possess clumsy body posture?

Foal-sure and big-footed he tumbles across the laminate. Shaky
flicker of sense up the spinal pathways. Synaptic leaps saying
move or *glide*. The effort of nerves to shape the body's urgencies
stuttering into what's stuck.

5. Does he arrange toys in rows?

Because design is a prism of the mind. Because placement is in relation
    to.
Because the polyglot of form needs order. Because blue car next to green
    car
next to red car all along the highway. Because the serpentine of die-cast
    metal
relentlessly gleams. Because form is relentless, relentlessly infinite.

6. Does he smell, bang, lick, or inappropriately use toys?

Unbuffered tang. Metallic with a murmur
of salt. An ersatz flavor fevering plastics.
Having tasted sugar. Having known
sugar when the knowing is a haunt.
A shape in the mouth that is not a soufflé
and not a seed. This palpable fat.
This gummy warmth.
This tender unknown.

7. Does he focus interest on toy parts such as car wheels?

Every object has a purpose. Every purpose hums its will.
Plastic tires in close orbits. Firestones nearly spun
into the eye. As if the urge to become the eye
was the tire's concern. The idea that the thing
could move beyond the membranes
of the self to become fully boy. To be sewn into
the boy's mind. And having been possessed intensely
by the thing, upon the thing's cessation, grief.

8. Is he obsessed with objects or topics?

The *Amanita* genus is his favorite and includes the "death cap."
You will know a death cap by its off-colored patches,
the remnants of what was once a veil that had surrounded
the mushroom when it was young. We had lived
in a place of quiet, surrounded by every manner of fungus,
and he would stand in the rain until drenched looking
at the same clump of mushrooms. Fairy rings. Polypore shelves.
Sleek and concealed little spore-bearers hidden under leaves.
Lobes of chanterelles. The coral-like hemispheres of morels
thinking in their darkness.

9. Does he spin objects, himself? Is he fascinated with spinning objects?

Pinwheels staked along the sidewalk.
Their abiding gyres a mess of colors. He seems
to take them as evidence of
the refuge. An embrace behind the eyes.
A wild ecstasy trammeled by a center. It hones him in.
His being wound down as one winds a clock to take
ample measure of what is infinitesimally
daunting and thus pulled in by the swirl.

10. Are his interests restricted? (Does he watch the same video over and over?)

In the dark. In the night. In the glow of the day. Audible fuzz
of the screen like passing rain. Shuddering spray of TV light.
Its pixelated filaments pierce the gloom, split the gap that veils
in from out. The image makes a testament that's constantly upheld.

11. Does he have difficulty stopping a repetitive "boring" activity or con-
versation?

The toy truck's wheels rotate clockwise then counter.
In the sandbox he puts his eyes close to the wheels; the sand
hisses out from the treads and into the tender folds
of his eye, its membrane's soft tissues. The pain
must be unbearable and still he pushes me away as I try
to reclaim him from whatever mystery holds him. From whatever
faraway place whistles to his brain—its boulevard of wheels
spinning past his bewildered imagination.

12. Does he have an unusual attachment to objects—sticks, stones, strings,
hair, etc.?

Pocketfuls of stone: chalcedony and pyrite. The milky ghost
of quartz. Tiger's eye. Iron flakes wedged into thin veins.
Ores reluctantly peering in tentacle-like threads, sewn into
igneous rhyolite. Peppered granites and rounded skipping stones
palmed and warm. He'd demand I carry them all in my pockets.
All of their weight pressed against my thigh, raucous with each step.

13. Is he stubborn about rituals and routines? Is he resistant to change?

Head down, his mind a needle. Intellect extended into
the tip where his concentration pierces the veil. A thousand
tiny exit wounds of time against the backdrop of the sun
become a galaxy. A galaxy of pinpricks where the seasons
never change and October is always October and the forms
of constellations are immutable. Never ebbing. Never
unreliably winking out like gods of firm promises.

14. Are his tastes restricted by consistency, shape or form?

His mouth cradles the form that is most consistent with a memory.

15. Does he have a savant ability or a restricted skill superior to his age group?

His mind teems with magical thought—
the possibilities of every moment: if the clock were a cicada
winding down; if the rain were an unfurled scroll of lost voices;
if the sky held all the animals everyone had loved, then
the absolutes holding us here with our grief are not sovereign.
That this alchemy, scratched with debris and errata, these waves
sweeping our houses loose from their pilings, all of it is soluble
in the swirling cacophony of his mind.

Chorus: Select an Answer

A. Inside the spiral of the canal, a shining table where the patient cannot be touched. A boy hums at a window and hears the hum murmur back at him as the glass rattles the way a dragonfly's cellophane wings shatter themselves in flight.

B. The window overlooks an audience.

C. The audience swigs their narcotics and looks down into the theater where a body lay open like a piazza, and the terrible light opens it further onto the stage where a language arranges and arranges, only able to keep the darkness still for a while.

D. The verb of the saw. The verb of the hand.

Episode 5

Labyrinth

The boy in the labyrinth catches sparks off pitchblende in the dark. Bright anthracite throws light at odd angles. Sulfur and earth. Mud caked on the undersides of the boy's soles. Here in the heart of the maze, senses lift the walls so that sounds flash their luminous flares in the shadow. Water droplets in mid-flight singe the air with the speed of their flight. Light passes with wafts of air through corridors. The boy's eyes have grown used to the dark. And so this little respite from it heaves a heavy weight on the boy. Time and time. Sun rays filter down from the ceiling. To signify. To seal the boy among the minerals.

He shouts loud vowels at the damp mineral deposits in the walls. His voice tries to pierce through the gloom. It trebles back, thick and high, mimics the gesture of the maze's discreet geology. And so the sound of him spills its waves into a disfigured future. His voice sieved on the rebound. As if compelled to shear itself of various layers. Sound parsed into other sounds. The tremolo. The angular anguish of a throated trill. Though sweetness fills his mouth, the earth concedes its own tangled brooding sidestep. Its own quotidian.

*

The boy reaches skyward. The boy in the sky does not reach back. Having stared at one another into the long dark, understandings between the two pass. Their shadows cross and uncross with the hours. Caverns define their figures as asters define their fields. Beginnings cross and uncross in spurious fashion. The boy in the labyrinth chips at a wall with the end of his torch until both wall and torch have marked each other. Tendrils of a vine curled around an arbor deface the arbor. A face looks into a face. Hands gesture toward other hands.

*

The boy in the labyrinth is tired of looking. There is a boy in the sky. The boy above coaxes his big shadow into a widening circle, encompassing the boy in the labyrinth. Between the two, an image—shadow over the face of one, shadow covering the body of the other. Sunlight behind the head of the boy in the sky, though obscured, is still sunlight. And flowers blooming inside the skull are still nasturtiums. The flower bursting from within an empty head is a flower bursting from within an empty head and nothing more. Looking further will not reveal anything. And so the boy in the sky does not leave to fetch help and the boy in the darkness, tired of asking, holds his knees to his chest and hums.

The boy hums. An old tune. A tune from a long dream. A dream with beasts, filled with the odor of cumin and turmeric. A yellowed melody heard from somewhere but he cannot remember, having spent so many days looking at the sky, losing his place in the maze. Smells of earth, thick and autumnal. And the soft red spiral wound around his wrist. The red yarn of his spent spool twangs its own nag in the hollows of the underworld. Perhaps, the boy thinks, the note breathed into its knots and tangles will sound out a path. Minor chords. An elegy. A dirge by one who moved by darkness, drawn to its black possibility.

*

There are possibilities in darkness: either the beast or not the beast. Either motion or stillness. Flowers push their heads through eye sockets. A little breath hushes the velvet black. God's eyes pierce the gloom. The boy thinks about the Minotaur's music and his own lost ball of string. Whether the nest at the heart of the maze sprouts other beasts. Other boys. Whether the possibilities know they are possibilities, rich and cold. The boy worries the light off his torch. Worries the scorched passageways. He thinks there are eyes that feel him pass. That we know each other through sparks in the dark.

He tears strips from his robe and coils them around the base of his torch for fire. He feeds the flame. And as the fire grows, so does his knowledge of the cold. The frayed ends of his threads wave like bare roots. The fire eats the air as lazy waves radiate in the haze. His bare thighs twitch. Chilled. In the darkness, a glint of his skin can be seen in the flash of his torch's light. The tunnels bear the heat-tongue of the newly fed flame in the blackened archways. And in the flicker, the red thump of the boy's heart leads the way.

The heart leads the next journey. Its thick systolic lurch. Its clear call from the carotid's shunt. Somewhere the Minotaur refuses to say hello. Somewhere lost moths beat themselves to death against a torch's reflection. The actual light somewhere, which is a silence between the boy and the beast. That understanding. That repetition of silences as when a light is switched on and off. The two of them quiet in the dark, listening to their own hearts pump, *law, law, law*. The boy thinks, *beast, if you can hear, this is my heart.* It thrums like a shirt full of plums plopped into a basket. *Dear beast, listen to my valves strike. Listen to them open.*

He listens keenly as one grown used to the dark. And in the spaces of his breathing, his spatial relations break as ice upon the sea. What sounds solid in front of him does not connect with what he sees. The connection to being lost as happening to one externally and internally. Just as beauty is a matter of value. The caverns where the boy is lost are beautiful, but in the darkness, he cannot see them. Therefore, they have become all the more beautiful. There are events and events, and there is something to mean. The boy's breath coming in circles extends with this belief: that there is beauty in the dark spaces. Hear its hoof. Hear its song.

Chorus: Solve for X

All night the hum of the X as it leaves the skin open a crack. Ink draws its slipstream across the broken X. Blood fills the rims of the depression. In black, first the edge, then X is a veined feather. The feather, a thing of the new world.

Slowly X rejects its new colors. Its facsimiles rippling like spirits from the corners of sleep.

How can it not be the only beauty? Wanting to feel the bite of X, dark and bluing just underneath what is felt.

Episode 6

Labyrinth

The boy in the labyrinth hears the Minotaur's song. Its intonation. Breath thick like deep reed-song. Deeper than inside the boy's belly. The drone of it. Night into day into night. The labyrinth summons songs from the ether. The boy watches slow and wide breezes fan cobwebs back, pull strands outward. Suck them back in. The whole cavern breathing. Blue notes of night passing into day shift the spider's diadem into a quickening glissando. How lovely the beast's voice, the boy thinks. Its low vowels hoarse. Its breath hemmed to the edges of the boy's eardrum.

The boy feels hemmed in. He is a chrysanthemum with its stem cross-stitched into the design of a curtain's fringe. The body, pressed against the dark, thus fulfills its gloss. A body, thus, carries with it what fades. Little hooks tug at the corners of the boy's skin. Little nudges paw at his head. The boy in the labyrinth feels each presence of the labyrinth equally except the beast's. The honey-sweet ooze of the beast's vowels, fierce in the dignity of the larynx's brass. The Minotaur's nearness swallows all the atmosphere. Its sound takes up the space all around the boy. Its sound tugs the knot.

*

His senses, contingencies—tugged as a single cord around a post. Because the red string was a dream of unity. Because the red string thinner than a spider's web was the abstraction, as toxic as any trick the mind tells itself. The parentheses of the string, unspooled into bright red bouquets criss-crossed into the dark's thicket. To the boy it is the grid of his life passing by. The brickworks at his feet tick and tick as he steps, pulls at the cord to bring him back. The intervals descend, a sequence of lists: here is the hole in the ceiling, and this is the nest. This is the war gallery, and this is where the bodies raised the level of the pond. The boy's hands, insatiable as he gathers it all in, falling forward with a song at his back.

Windows open to other windows. He winds the red string around his wrist. Held by the soft red manacle, he rolls backwards toward the reeling light. Shoulders rise as if offered to the beast. The song at the boy's back—*Oh, Minotaur, Minotaur,* he sings. All the outlines of the wall edges are soft, bitten by water. Light cuts the boy's body into tiny seams. Such friction as he moves, chased by an imperative. Above, the boy imagines fields under stars. Late doves flap and flap, awoken out of sleep as children run across their expanse. *Oh, Minotaur, Minotaur, Minotaur.* Its hard breaths circulate. Bring the boy back. Remind.

How the word laces the dark in knots. Ties itself into the fabric of the air. *Oh, Minotaur, Minotaur,* the boy sings. Buoyant words. They rise toward light like vines. And the red manacled thread, gathered, weighs heavily on the boy's wrist. The thread governs his pulse. Begins to grow. The boy in the labyrinth hears himself hum as one coming to love. When the heart has ears, the tender places shift. The boy's heart rising from his wrist into the lacy red. The world, uncanny with omissions. Swoon pours into swoon. And the string that trails into the darkness moves the boy's body through.

To guard against the physics of the dark one must make one's self small. Each body in space is accusatory. Mass attracts mass—to remain insignificant, the boy must hold his limbs close to his core. Certain coefficients lack the details of what or whom they multiply. Large beasts in the darkness are, therefore, amplified. This the boy knows: the sounds drawn inward into the ear pull the breath of the landscape into cellular meanings. The gravity of the beast's strident song draws in the boy's red threads. Draws in the boy's heartbeat.

*

His heart sifts through the morning's weight. The life promised resides somewhere in the hungry marrow. The promised life becomes something else....In the surface world they've planted trees ahead of summer. The crust shakes off the remaindered mulch and reveals crocus. A steady stipple of asphodel. From the heart to the mind, the weary boy feels his blood crochet a lacy sequence of misinformation. Asphodel, asphodel, asphodel: the mind counts its wreck in beautiful and urgent wishes. Here in the dark the shifting valves of the heart make and make.

The boy feels the shape of the thing he's made. Along its back the staggered spine adheres to its downward path from the base of the beast's neck to its pelvic girdle. The heavy spine choreographs the pivot from the hip to the skull. Bull horns jut in a steady consideration of their weight. The pole that adjusts the tightrope walker distributes the athlete's gravity to her center. The shape of the thing has a function. The function of terror is to instruct. The function of applause is to laud. The shape of the thing grows as it approaches the boy's torch. Therefore, its shadow grows as the proximity to a source of light diminishes. In the labyrinth, there is constantly the problem of proximity. How what is understood about where you stand depends on where you stand.

Chorus: Complete the Sentences

Even the drink of it _____ boundaries. The sweet tribunal of cold against a parched throat. Then laughter sweeps the dream into the grass.

The upshoots of thirst are miserable finches, loud firings of feathered atoms into the maw. Into the suppose.

Suppose the sweet bubbled over the desert from a pierced stone. Suppose there was enough for us all, for the mothers with baskets on their backs filled with children.

Think, then, of the _____ of drought and the apricot still drying on the sill. Think on it and turn the spigot until it gets going again.

A. throttles...stupidity
B. imagines...complexities
C. realizes...hazard
D. quenches...loveliness

Episode 7

Labyrinth

The boy in the labyrinth knows everything depends on where you stand. What is in the foreground defies the background in exaggerated lines. As light shined behind parchment grows the wrought letters into rivers, heavy with the profundities of their lineation. How sunlight strikes an apple tree and how the weight of that tree swells the outward feel of its fat and beautiful fruit. The scale is not a concept. It is a veil. The boy in the labyrinth knows the array. His concentration compressed by the boundaries where he is concerned: his body and his body. All others are relative. He imagines his body as a sheet of blackened glass. How his senses are seen through it if one peers.

*

From behind his fingers, small beams of light cross his iris. Light sheds its act through the boy's rock-toughened knuckles. His sleep deficit calls him to the stage so that under the lights he is misrecognized. A stormy self, analogous to the boy's idea of physical beauty. How the landscape determines or dominates the content. Therefore, the Minotaur is beautiful in the dark. Therefore, the boy is beautiful in the dark. Therefore, the labyrinth is razored into pieces between the boy's fingers. The dream which had existed still swells in an opera house.

Inside an opera house, swells of music glow blue and ionize the air. He delicately rotates his hands in tune to his emotion, which is like a dwelling. In here he dwells, he thinks, as his hands twirl into sad feelings. It is the beauty of the Minotaur's song that is derived from a single fact—within a song someone is present. With every note there is transference. As when wind from spinning hands substitutes actual wind. As when the reed of a throat does not require an audience. As when the audience is far from the stage and the stage stammers its incongruity.

A polyglot of voices fills his head. Point-to-point, words accrue. Materials pile until his thought is no longer a solid thing. As when the silhouettes of horses stampede in a back-lit cloudburst. As when the plane of his thought separates from the planes of spaces between labyrinthine walls. He cannot relate it to something, the words forming at the back of his throat. The word he is gathering to say is far from the stage. The word he is gathering to say is spacious. A collation of shadow and seam, the protuberances patch an invisible pain. A horizon forms around his stammer. Time goes there. Time concentrates on the boy's sound.

To make oneself frightfully small in the face of imminent danger...to collapse into one's beating heart. To eschew the body takes a toll. So the boy imagines that sanctuary is a dwelling, safe below his insides. He imagines its white-lined walls, bedecked in candles and warmth. The dark smudge of smoke residue resides in the periphery, black and corpulent. But here is safety. Here is the frontier, steady and incremental. There is no beast place in the within. There is no room for the hooves. No room for such animal violence.

*

Each door opens to another door. Each passageway winds and winds, snakes into the deep cortical recesses of memory. And each memory is its own serpent. Each memory is its own spear tip twisted into the boy's body. Down one passageway, a tree-lined cobble drive. Down another, an olive tree drops its pits, leaves a mash of black blossom to thicken and ooze. How beautiful these corridors with their shut doors. How beautiful this empty house turning in its own shaky air.

*

Perhaps the cavern receding, one passage into the next, cannot contain the boy as he tornados in place. How spun, the world. The rooms of the maze are adorned identically. And among the identical rooms, perhaps god dwells. Perhaps the beast dwells, having multiple nests. And in such dwellings, the boy is spun—eyes dart right to left, right to left. The wheel of his breath leaves his body. Rises up from his chest out of his mouth. The soft salt at the edge of his lips cooled into a gritty cake. The labyrinth turns in circles and multiplies its falsity.

The boy has no memory of this place. It's as if night had just fallen and what is understood laces into the underground streams. What is understood recedes in the cold distance. At this point, the way is forgotten. At this point, what is distal and what is proximal are indistinct. What the boy feels inside sets a spike into his jaw. His tender mouth, bitten. Teeth drive their edges against his cheek. Hollow. The boy feels hollowed out. As if a dogwood blossom, filled with implicit promises, had been turned wrong side out. How the error of what is on the inside is held outward and raw. And still the heavy kick drum of the bull-man's gait shakes the boy's gut. Still the labyrinth gathers its boundaries in redundant corridors.

Redundant corners. Jags and outcroppings cast sharp shadows against themselves. The quarried marble of the netherworld taken back to the surface leaves all the glamour of a mouth. And the salt is fresh upon the boy's lips. The salt is a consistent taste. It's stirred from the minerals dripping from the limestone stalactites. Still, the boy knows that he is not with the sea. Here, there are fat, decorous phantoms which shred thin light from the boy's torch into vigorous impastos. Shadow upon black upon shadow. And what riches reside here gleam to an interior treble.

Chorus: Monster Is to Damned as Lariat Is to _____

Asphalt, then lariat. The rope drags its wet silhouette into a trail of wounds. Little sidewinding torsos flashed in curlicues.

Sibilances between a record of low voices. Low hisses insisting on its "yes." Its omnipotent "yes." Around the knot, the slickened knuckle, tight against its groove, shirring strands adjacent.

The braid like rivulets against a window. The wet span of the noose splits what is done into undone.

A Story Problem

A cart carrying a metric ton of apples leaves the city at four meters per second. Another cart leaves the city carrying a boy, in love with an idea. Consider the swirl of laughter and personal tragedy at six meters per second. Say the idea does not love him back. Say he will lose his life in a maze of regrets. What can be said about the dust caked on the wheel spokes and the precarious sway of the chassis crossing over ruts and the staggered pavers knuckled together side by side? At four meters per second, is there enough time to sample what is carried? Say the apples find their way into the basket of a family a dozen miles away before the boy gets there. Where did he stop? Did he consider the essence of the problem? If the distance of love is coupled by the weight of an apple cart bound for the markets or bazaars of a city as far away as autumn, then what can be said about the horses who will never taste their burden? Where will his cart pass the adenoidal fruits along the road? Where will he know the plurality of his blood?

Epode

Autism Screening Questionnaire: Speech and Language Delay

1. Did your child lose acquired speech?

A fount and then silence. A none. An ellipse
between—his breath through
the seams of our windows. Whistle
of days. Impossible bowl of a mouth—
the open cupboard, vowels
rounded up and swept under the rug.

2. Does your child produce unusual noises or infantile squeals?

He'd coo and we'd coo back. The sound
passed back and forth between us like a ball.
Or later, an astral voice. Some vibrato
under the surface of us. The burst upon—
burn of strings rubbed
in a flourish. His exhausted face.

3. Is your child's voice louder than required?

In an enclosure or a cave, it is difficult to gauge
one's volume. The proscenium of the world.
All the rooms we speak of are dark places. Because
he cannot see his mouth, he cannot imagine
the sound that comes out.

4. Does your child speak frequent gibberish or jargon?

To my ears it is a language. Every sound
a system: the sound for *dog* or *boy*. The moan
in his throat for water—that of a man with thirst.
The dilapidated ladder that makes a sentence
a sentence. This plosive is a verb. This liquid
a want. We make symbols of his noise.

5. Does your child have difficulty understanding basic things ("just can't
get it")?

Against the backdrop of the tree he looks so small.

6. Does your child pull you around when he wants something?

By the sleeve. By the shirttail. His light touch
hopscotching against my skin like sparrows.
An insistence muscled and muscled again.

7. Does your child have difficulty expressing his needs or desires using
gestures?

Red-faced in the kitchen and in the bedroom,
and the yellow light touches his eyes
which are open but not there. His eyes
rest in their narrow boat dream, and the canals
are wide dividing this side from this side.

8. Is there no spontaneous initiation of speech or communication from your child?

When called he eases out of his body.
His god is not our words nor is it
the words from his lips. It is entirely body.
So when he comes to us and looks we know
there are beyond us impossible cylinders
where meaning lives.

9. Does your child repeat heard words, parts of words, or TV commercials?

The mind circles the mind in the arena, far in—far in
where the consonants touch and where the round
chorus flaunts its iambs in a metronomic trot. Humming
to himself in warm and jugular songs.

10. Does your child use repetitive language (same word or phrase over and over)?

A pocket in his brain worries its ball of lint.
A word clicks into its groove and stammers
along its track, Dopplering like a car with its windows
rolled down, and the one top hit of the summer
angles its way into his brain.

11. Does your child have difficulty sustaining a conversation?

We could be anywhere, then the navel of the red moon
drops its fruit. His world. This stained world drips its honey
into our mouths. Our words stolen from his malingering afternoon.

12. Does your child use monotonous speech or wrong pausing?

When the air is true and simple, we can watch him tremble
for an hour, plucking his meaning from a handful of utterances,
and then ascend into the terrible partition of speech.

13. Does your child speak the same to kids, adults, or objects (can't differentiate)?

Because a reference needs a frame: we are mother and father
and child with a world of time to be understood. The car radio
plays its one song. The song, therefore, is important.
It must be intoned at a rigorous time. Because rigor
is important and because the self insists on constant vigils.

14. Does your child use language inappropriately (wrong words or phrases)?

Always, and he insists on the incorrect forms.
The wrong word takes every form for love—
the good tree leans into the pond,
the gray dog's ribs show, the memory
bound to the window, and the promise of the radio
playing its song on the hour. Every wrong form
is a form which represents us in our losses,
if it takes us another world to understand.

Chorus: Mongrel Is to Madness as Fire Is to _____

A fire moved, taking warmth with it. Unthinkable, its cargo. It mirrored birds in their fatal plumes. Too heavy to fly, they drag the weight of themselves, beautifully.

As the fire trembles with motion, the fever also moves with a surprise like joy. Like a season on the brink of cool, yet holding. Holding on.

Let me say that all that brilliance held me. Alarmed me. Betrayed all my verbs.

Episode 8

Labyrinth

The boy in the labyrinth understands the treble. Understands what peals from the interior. The door arches, and lapsed passageways stretch beyond. And what collapses with the distance is the truest sound. The sound's purity stretched thin as red thread pulled taut from a spool. How the spool's weight dissipates as though the weight was taken up by the air. Oh, how the air feels to the boy, as the note rings clear in his ears. How heavy and salty the air. He can feel the ocean sifting between the caverns. Can feel the tides pull at the stone sides as the foundation of where he stands recedes and recedes.

*

Light recedes from his torch. The strip of cloth bound tightly to the head of a stick. The wick's fuel slips in sappy lozenges. Small knuckles of fuel flame on in ellipsis. The way lit as if in mid-thought. And what else recedes? The feel of salt and ocean mist on the boy's face. The idea that beneath it all resides an ocean. Within the earth's belly. Within the boy. And here he would find the Minotaur, sullen, bored. His lungs filled with silica and ground human bone. The flicker of light tosses bits of his head in thick black shadows. Those shadows deepening to outrageous depths.

Shadows deepen. The outrage of their movements mimics the torch's flame. Embers snap from the centers in extravagant suicides. And the beast stirs. The beast, who is half a body, gives himself over to rage. The aeolian center cradles his roar. Pushes it through its cylindrical hallways so that the beast's sound carries mass. And his animal shout cleaves the bedding-plane into flakes of sharp sediment that hum. Chipped rocks shift along their flat sides. It is a low sound the beast makes. A song in low registers.

*

The boy hears a deep song. It is a comfort, but cold as the bottom of glacial ice. He stumbles through the maze, and still the tune hangs from the stalactites. A film glistens from the flame he holds aloft. The after-echo from the flame tongue at the end of his torch scratches a charcoal line into the corridor. The torch's reply, liquid, mixed with the sound of his footfall in the narrows of the path. The boy imagines that tonight, in the surface world, rain falls upon houses. Sewers swell with bits of clay, turn gutter waters red. The runoff spills into tributaries here under ground. He imagines the frogs will sing. Imagines they will hum.

A tune from memory to keep the time at bay. Something electric. A singe of energy twists from the crucible of his lips, arcs from doorway to door-way. A puff of air into the air. It blooms from the boy's mouth. Radiates into a white, translucent berry. It swells before his eyes and loses its form in the darkness. There are blind fish here. Animals born without eyes. They feel the boy's breath along their sides as it writhes along the contours of their forms. Each note of the boy's song on their spines slides down the length of them. The boy feels them too. Their insomniac forms lean into his hum's sweet kiss.

*

Cave-ins from somewhere in the tunnels send gusts of wind into the boy's face. The boy imagines a wheel spins in his brain to make the cavern shake. The rhythm of it turns in the spirals of the boy's ear. Sound made thicker in the dark. Sound, absolute—a pitch heightened by the boy's hunger. The fury of his mind honed from the underground, he thinks he hears wind through the pinnate wings of gulls far above the tunnels. Imagines a cart above, heavy with fruit for the afternoon bazaars. He dreams his teeth piercing a plucked grape's skin. Incisors splitting in half the soft brown seed. His mind stretches beyond its elastic point. Bends to what the dark gives.

*

The boy closes his eyes. Imagines that the darkness lies to him. Because it is full of lies. Because at the center of the darkness is a man who is also a bull. And he is curled up at the hub of it all. The boy thinks about the man-bull padding his way along the slick corridors, rubbing his sides against the hewn edges of basalt. Here and there a tuft of fur snags, yanked out in patches. The Minotaur nudges along the way the sightless fishes swim up with the waters of the underworld, pulled by the current, the waters sucked through their mouths and on through their gills. To the fish, it's as if the current were a thing with a mind. It enters the mouth and leaves it according to its will. And in the labyrinth the will is forever wishing to be let in.

*

The boy feels water in his mouth. Inside the chambers of his heart, the cold holds him tightly. He takes a drink and feels it travel down his esophagus into his stomach. It pools there. Eddies. The cylindrical tunnels curl into other rooms. The other rooms house possibilities. And between sips, there is breath. There is muscle. Depth. In the labyrinth, there are wishes. Wishes and doorways. The boy's body and the labyrinth within.

He opens doors and peers into the archways—rooms with cool and constant colors. Frogs assault the cavern with their assertions. *Here. Here. I am here.* The boy in the labyrinth searches for a name. For the beast. But these are not a name. Nothing but totems and wonder. And to the palpitations of frog song the boy dreams. Lovely faraway things like peonies idle in the boy's brain. Lobes of the flowers rise, explode, and decay with the throaty vowels. A name cleaves its heart into the pyrite of the cavern. Its red soul seers him when he blinks. Nothing else pierces his dream. Nothing else except the canals of his inner ear doubling in its spiral. The sound of a name orphaned in the cold.

Chorus: Select an Answer

A. Dust in the light shaft was surely lost. Surely the alternative to looking.

B. If there is too much to keep us tired, then there's too much to keep from us. A promise, for example. A life of watching.

C. The brittle time when my heart asked for a way to free itself. It could be that the horizon is lonely. It could be that the children in the playground stain their clothes. The girl with the smooth face and the denim dress smeared with berries and the good talk of the mothers.

D. All the useless hooks humming with their empty teeth.

Episode 9

Labyrinth

The boy in the labyrinth thinks the mysteries of the maze are mysteries because there are no windows. The insides are all sewn shut. So when the boy feels something, really feels it, he knows it is a thing not to be given up. It is a thing to remember and to constantly ask, *Am I awake? Am I awake?* The answer is in all directions. The tunnels fork into smaller and smaller tunnels. The cicadas sing their paradiddle. A door is pried open. A heart is run through with a spear. All these possibilities turn the compass rose upside down. What's left of the boy's sense of direction floats upward with the bull-man's hot breath.

The boy wanders inside the bull's hot breath. Each curl of mist, a blue room. Each room bears a door. A circle of a doorknob, warm to the touch. The warmth like someone having lived in the boy's space for an age. All over the cave, remnants of body heat throb off of the corridors. A mongrel heat. Morning-heavy, arrested in the intake of air through nostrils deep like the very caverns that hold the beast. Inside the Minotaur's breath, a room he can sleep inside. A room he can hone.

He sets his lips to the floor. Hard wet kisses rise back from the stone. *I want something like the mind breaking into slivers*, he thinks. Bread's hard rind bitten to tinder. Glandular risings from behind the jowls. Mouth full of saliva to lather the tongue into a muscular pain. A spasm of body. He kisses the ground and feels his pulse tugged in his throat as his blood searches for something in its vascular dark. Blood's little sips along his insides.

A subterranean lake swallows its single crop. Water droplets from stalactites uncoil along the grooves of each tooth like impromptu tributes. The way stacked stones mark death on remote roads. Wind sweeps its angles and scolds the outcrops. Wears them smooth. The boy stands as still as he can. The world—it cannot be still, knowing what it knows. Inside the world, its core writhes in its desire to be a star. In its knowing, it will never.

*

The beauty of fever. The beauty of hot red breaths brought in and in. Little red strides traipsing through the cold air. Tonight, the boy is tired. Tonight along the sides of the underworld, water, and its strange compulsion, seeks its terminus in something. It doesn't know. It doesn't know the names of things, just the resistance to its desire. Sometimes misery is beautiful, the boy thinks. To afford the dream, misery holds in its fist. To afford the bright red cherries spilling from the hand that brings them up from a paper bag.

*

Autumnal in his paces, he feels the deep tongue of stone nudge at his ankle. He feels the eaves in the surface world fill with rain and the leaves awash in the streets. They clot the alleyways causing water to pool in persistent fevers. The beast in the maze is awash in shadow. Memory is a speckled pear skin. The boy and the beast sleep in quarters distant from each other, yet through the stone the sound of water is curdled breaths.

*

The boy in the labyrinth remembers summer. He remembers light along a bridge. Its frame lit like an instrument. A sweating body. And how the people crossed its back, shouldering baskets of fruit. How the light shone on the dappled skins of pears. Apricots. Whole mountains of sweets to ease the tongue into a new century. And because the boy is here, in the dark, his tongue is dangerous. It leads him, slipping down into himself. Past all sense of things. Past hunger filled up on memory's cup.

The boy in the labyrinth remembers drums. Noise ricocheting from the skin into his chest. How his basket of ribs felt his heart spin around. A windmill path. Against the noise, he had stood with his eyes closed as his breath throttled out of him. The shape of his body seemingly squeezed out of the circle of his mouth. And in the void, without any other sound or light, the pulse of blood from behind his ears becomes the footsteps of *his* interruption. He. The face that is the hole at the center of the boy. Its leaving face. Its god face. The beast in his most glorious hefts his lungs forward.

He listens to the keen sound of water droplets strike their tinny notes. His tympanic membrane devours the sound wave. A drop from a goblet spilled to a sponge. Other sounds. Keratin scratched against limestone. Sparks from fur brushed against the outcroppings. Even the smallest click of teeth against the impossible seed misplaced here in the dark. Even the heartbeat. Especially the heartbeat from deep within his throat.

*

The boy doesn't call it fear. He doesn't call it anything. Just a feeling that starts as small as a child's red cup held close to the chest. Cradled. Warmed by the heart's lambent engine. Rather than a cup, could it be a bird? A rook, all wayward and shuddering. Wild-eyed in the dark wineskin of the boy's body. Or is his pulse no pulse at all, but an expectation? Like the company pain keeps. Like the half-man, half-bull running the length of his paddock wondering about the symmetry of his horns and the weight he bears.

Chorus: Solve for X

And in the outer world, the first, something smooth and wet. An X skims across the tops of the crests in a succession of skips. The longest holds its space in the air, pauses, then descends into what is a cool sleep.

X and all the faces of backlit animals gaze downward at you. Their curious engulfed silhouettes. A spasm of radio and the accident of understanding what it means to be X. What it means to be held and kissed and gibbered to as though you were something cast away and suddenly, miraculously, returned.

Episode 10

Labyrinth

The boy in the labyrinth feels his irises widen. They have rippled into the blackest water. To watch a sunrise now would hammer his brain beyond what the world could contain. There would not be enough rooms where he could hide. He goes onward, hands in front of his face. The torch long since extinguished, though the sounds of its hunger still click in his ear. Straight and swift he moves. Feels his way through the dimensions of the cavern. Hears the drool of the beast drip on cooled granite. The boy's eyes, so beautiful and deep. Secluded in the recesses of his sockets. Swallowed in an enfolding thirst.

*

The boy cups his hands around stilled water and takes a deep sip. Feels the water thrill down his throat. What a wonder, he thinks, to feel the cold inside him. He hears his esophagus close. Little valves of his body open and shut. Inside him, water threads out into other pathways. His thirst disperses as water floods his stomach. And on the inside, he is calmed. He listens further and deeper into the colonnades of the underground. Columns hold the surface world up. Row upon row of columns. He feels he is beneath a giant animal's ribs. That he is the water that runs beneath.

*

He cannot speak of what he feels, only that the syntax of water fills his elastic memory up to his eyes—events in relation to the failure of his voice, having wandered silently for so long. And in the chill, the dark thickens into the thickest velvet. The pitch of it, soft, and the light slosh of his feet in the water urges him forward. The dark is the texture of fur, and the curtain slides back. He is in the theater of his skull. And in the theater of his skull, the half-bull snorts its sonata. Day after idiomatic day passes. The bull-man's hum charges ahead of the wave inside the boy's brain. Everything the boy feels is intolerable and persists.

Talk to me, he thinks. He never hears an answer. Nothing fills the grammar he desires except the labyrinth's elaborate hoaxes. A door opens into a wall. The wall conceals another wall. Beyond that, spent flowers in need of dead-heading in some place above. A chasm. A river. A rudderless song about the afterlife. About time. To the boy, the surface world is so spent. He is tired of dreams and the red string's dye sluiced through his hands. The stage of the boy's mind is devised into lobes of meaning. None of which he can see. None of which the beast sees unless he were to eat the boy. An intolerable end, the boy thinks. One more silence. One more closed closet door.

One more door. One more doctored space in the space of the now. On the floor, he sees bottles, bones, a stoppered flask. He sees cracked earthenware and the smudge of char on the wall. On and on, beyond the door are other doors—a farthering off like that trick of mirrors. One mirror held up to another opening into mirrors inside the mirror. Each image lacerates time. Makes the space of residency an object. His eyes adjust to the multiplicity and he sees the beast's sleeping face. He hears its face breathe in deep tendrils of myth.

The boy is wrapped deep within. The sleeping beast's face, a reflection of his own. A mirror within a mirror into infinity. When he tilts his head to the side to regard the beast's horns, the space between the two of them curves. It is as if the two of them are falling together down a long shaft with row after row of doors. Doors that lead to other myths. Doors that open to nothing but air. The boy facing the beast feels the beast's grandeur. Its broad chest rises and falls as its breath fills the room with mist. A little fog hovers at the boy's ankles. It crawls along the stones. Takes the form of the walkways and halls. Its garrulous movements pump and retract with the Minotaur's respiration.

*

The boy's hand retracts from under the beast's snout. His hand, damp from its breath. The beast is an imprisoned form, the boy thinks. Forged from what is and of course the fears from above. It wanders here in the maze, trapped in the decayed soil of the sounding box. The boy runs his hands along the beast's body. The hairs of its matted hide rise to meet the boy's flesh. Beside the beast, he is a miniature. His quality, absolute beside the mountainous being. The boy balances his body. His left arm leans against the sleeping bull-man while he sets himself upright. He sees in the beast's palms a tangle of red twine. The beast in fetal position, curled around another maze.

*

The boy wonders at the shape of the Minotaur's inner ear—its labyrinthine tubes spiral into smaller and smaller tubes. It is the nature of artifacts to have fractures, missing pieces, an errant image rubbed raw against the weather. And here, the beast's ear is missing part of a lobe. The boy puts his hand on the wound. Feels the hardened edge of it, which yields to the velvety soft parts not maimed by sword or the panicked nails of victims. The boy rubs the beast's ear. Pinches the tissue between his thumb and middle finger. And the beast stirs a little. It moves. Its fur rising and falling between the boy's soft strokes.

*

Breaths rise and fall. He sees the contours of its human body as a form. Each line connects and belongs to the Minotaur the way the boy owns his own face. The way the scar on the boy's thigh aches to tell its story. The real thing substitutes what once was in the boy's memory. The real is flesh and is not a contingency. *How old are you?* the boy wonders as he feels the beast's sides. Skin tags mottle its furred parts. Little lumps serve as a disjunction. To the boy the beast feels like his hand touching his hand.

*

The boy feels his hand touch his own hand—gesture not unlike a handshake, the warmth spilling over from one side to the other. Within that handshake, he feels his own body. No, it is not a handshake. The boy's arms embrace himself. They are holding him up to face the Minotaur, asleep at the center of the labyrinth. The boy's arms cross. Form a double space—what is within and without their embrace. Everything external to their grasp is a desire. Everything within their clutches is a desire. The boy feels tossed in the middle of an errand. He wants to cross his arms around the Minotaur. The boy feels he is in a state of urgency. For it seems love is a spiritual exercise full of inferences and lingering.

Coda

A Story Problem

If a boy in the dark were to take three steps per second forward and if there were a coil of string approximately 100 yards in length rolled in the opposite direction. If there were a shadow moving at two steps per second toward a sound. Footfall or breath. If the string were red and spun from the soft wool of his mother's lambs, the ones who call softly at night to each other from the paddocks, having been frightened by thunder. If the string were dyed in a lamb's blood. Or if the thunder were instead wolves fanning out, belly-low in the wet grass. If there were no thunder and if there were no wolves, how many more steps until the boy reaches his destination? Until lightning sparks dry tinder? Until the wolves sink their jaws around the soft throat of the weakest lamb? And what if there were no string but a wire? And if that wire were nerves? A spasm of X if you're solving for X. Then what kind of journey is this having moved so little? Having known the wolves are in the dark. Knowing the string is too short. What then? If then?

One Labyrinth

I have wandered in to see him writing music for his trumpet. His head is low, close to his papers. The spirals of the treble clef close to his ear—nearly becoming his ear.

***

And then he rises to play. Notes in his hand rise and fall in scales. They are tracks in a snow-bitten page. He is a page of his symphony, beyond a single note.

***

He hears the music constantly. He hears it part stone. Vertices of sound waves pressing their tongues against hewn walls. There, in the dark, scales are played.

***

I am here because he has asked me to watch. He has practiced and can play confidently, and yes, he is skilled. His song is not obscenity but clearly, beautifully, song.

***

He is practicing his notes, ascending and descending through the valves of his trumpet. Veined lines of songs from the heart of something untraceable.

***

Air sluices through the curling brass. Breath through the mouthpiece. Breath through the valves. Breath through the bell.

***

His song parts stones. His song rends the labyrinthine passageways of his trumpet in a flourish. A movement rises from the center of his diaphragm.

***

False starts and false loves. From the center of the boy's mind a light is visible. And there where the maw leads to melt a clear pealing note.

Acknowledgments

Grateful acknowledgment to the editors and readers of the following journals, magazines, and anthologies in which these poems first appeared, often under different titles or in different forms:

Academy of American Poets Poem-A-Day, The Account, Anti-, At Length, The Bakery, Black Tongue Review, Columbia Poetry Review, The Common, A Congeries, Cream City Review, DIAGRAM, Fiction SE, Indiana Review, JMWW, The Journal, The Laurel Review, Mid-American Review, Midway Journal, The Offending Adam, Poetry Magazine, Poetry Northwest, Quarterly West, Salt Hill, The Seattle Review of Books, Sweet: A Literary Confection, Third Coast, Tupelo Quarterly, Zòcalo Public Square.

"Labyrinth 1," "Labyrinth 2," "Labyrinth 3," and "Labyrinth 4" also appeared in *All of Us—Sweet: The First Five Years.* Ed. Katherine Riegel. Sweet Publications, 2014.

"Autism Screening Questionnaire—Speech and Language Delay" also appears in *The Pushcart Prize XLIII: Best of the Small Presses 2019.* Ed. Bill Henderson. Pushcart Press, 2019.

"Chorus: Select an Answer" also appears in *The Eloquent Poem.* Ed. Elise Paschen. Persea Press, 2019.

Also, to my early readers, colleagues, and friends: Rick Barot, Bruce Beasley, Jennifer Chang, Sarah Gambito, Rigoberto González, Matthew Guenette, Carol Guess, Tiana Kahakuwila, Joseph Legaspi, Adrian Matejka, Erika Meitner, Vikas Menon, Brenda Miller, Aimee Nezhukumatathil, Suzanne Paola, Leila Phillip, Emilia Phillips, Jon Pineda, Stephanie Reents, Kathryn Trueblood, and Patrick Rosal.

To the beautiful people at the University of Akron Press—Mary Biddinger, Amy Freels, Jon Miller, Thea Ledendecker, Julie Gammon, and Westley the Dread Pirate Roberts. Poetry Lives!

To my chosen family, Kundiman, and to my parents. Blessings.

Many thanks to Rosalyn Driscoll, her dynamic sculptures, and her collaborative spirit.

Thanks to Western Washington University and the College of the Holy Cross for their generous support.

To all the care providers, special education teachers, autism specialists, and service advocates, and to the parents who know and who have shared.

Most of all, through thick and thin, to Meredith, L, N, and H.

Photo: Danielle Papandrea

Oliver de la Paz is the author of five books of poetry and coedited *A Face to Meet the Faces: An Anthology of Contemporary Persona Poetry*. A founding member of Kundiman, he teaches at the College of the Holy Cross and in the Low Residency MFA Program at Pacific Lutheran.

Printed in the United States
By Bookmasters